ASCENDING FROM ADVERSITY

IN THE WAKE OF A SILENT STORM

Sneha Jain

INDIA • SINGAPORE • MALAYSIA

ISBN 979-8-89588-698-4

To every untold story, every unshared tear, and every unyielding heart. Keep shining, keep dreaming, and never forget the power of your truth.

Introduction

In the quiet corners of our hearts lie unsaid feelings—whispers of longing, fear, and hope that often go unvoiced. Each of us carries a unique tapestry of experiences woven together by moments of joy and threads of pain. Yet, it is the unspoken struggles that often shape us most profoundly, marking our paths in ways that are both invisible and deeply felt.

Ascending from Adversity invites you to delve into these hidden emotions to explore the silent battles we wage within ourselves. It speaks to the ache of unexpressed sorrow and the flicker of hope that persists even in the darkest times.

Here, you'll find stories that resonate with the unarticulated truths we all hold—the moments when we felt alone in a crowded room, the times we masked our pain with a smile and the small victories that often go unnoticed. This book is a sanctuary for those who have grappled with their feelings but found the strength to rise. As we journey together, may you feel the warmth of shared understanding and the power of connection. You are not alone in your silence; your feelings matter, and your journey is worthy of recognition. Let's take this path together, ascending from the depths of our hearts toward a brighter, more authentic existence.

Dear Readers,

I've wandered through deserts where hope felt like a mirage, walked barefoot on shards of broken dreams, and stood at the edge of cliffs where the winds of doubt threatened to push me over. The storms I've faced weren't just rain - they were tempests, relentless and unforgiving, trying to wash away the pieces of me I was struggling to hold onto. But even in the darkest nights, I found stars hiding in the corners of the sky. I became the fire that refused to be extinguished, the tree that grew stronger with every gust of wind. I didn't ask for these battles, but I learned to embrace them, for it's in the cracks and scars that my strength was born. I am not just a survivor of adversity - I am the one who chose to rise above it, shaping my own path from the ashes.

As you read these words, I hope they resonate with you, even though part of me aches knowing they might. If you see yourself reflected in these lines—if my battles feel like your own—I want you to know that I understand. I wrote this because sometimes, the weight of unsaid feelings is too much to bear, and in these pages, you may find pieces of the silence you've been holding. I feel the sadness too, that familiar ache, but perhaps through my words, your untold story can finally breathe.

I've come to see being the odd one out as a
Badge of honour; it means I'm not afraid to be true to myself
in a world of masks.

"You saw me as the odd one out, the one who didn't quite fit into your neat little boxes. Every time you overlooked me, dismissed me, or whispered behind my back; you unknowingly stoked a fire within me. I felt every cold shoulder and every side glance, and instead of breaking, I decided to burn. I set myself ablaze with determination, with passion, with a hunger to prove that being different wasn't a weakness, but my greatest strength. You might have thought you could keep me in the shadows, but it was in those shadows that I found the spark to light my own path. I didn't just survive—I thrived. I turned your doubt into my fuel, your exclusion into my motivation. So, thank you, really. Because without your attempts to make me feel small, I might never have realised just how powerful I could become."

You only remembered me when your universe unravelled, yet I was silently stitching together my own shattered fragments.

I became my own light in a world that never stops dimming.

"How could you, my friend in all but heart, turn the blade against me when I trusted you with my deepest fears and dreams? We were two halves of the same heartbeat, weren't we? Inseparable in laughter, sharing secrets in the dead of night like whispered wishes to the stars. I thought you understood my silences and knew the language of my soul better than anyone. But now I see that while I was building bridges, you were quietly crafting knives. How could you smile at me, all the while hiding your intentions behind that warm façade? I wonder if you knew the impact if you understood that betrayal from you felt like an earthquake, shattering the foundation of who I thought I could trust. Did it ever cross your mind, the cost of your choice? Or did you think I wouldn't notice the coldness creeping in, the shadows you cast on our once-sunny days? I still remember the good times and the laughter that felt like it would never end. How do I reconcile those memories with the sharp pain of your betrayal? I find myself asking if you were ever really the friend I thought you were or if I was just too blind to see the cracks in your loyalty. Yet, here I am, piecing myself back together, trying to make sense of the puzzle you've left behind. Was it worth it for you? Was your choice to hurt me worth losing the bond we once had? I may never understand why you chose to backstab instead of stand beside me, but I'm learning that maybe this was the lesson I needed to find the strength to let go and heal."

I was the contingency you turned to when all your other priorities crumbled.

Your praise always felt like a blade wrapped in velvet,
soft until it cuts.

"Why do I build these walls so high, locking every door in my mind at the first sign of a storm? Why does my heart race like a wild horse at the slightest hint of judgement, thundering in my chest as if chased by unseen shadows? I wonder how I became this fortress, guarded and wary, with every crack sealed tight.

But amidst the chaos inside, I still find myself smiling, don't I? Despite the fear, despite the weight of a thousand whispered doubts, I walk through each day with a kind of quiet defiance. Maybe that's my strength—the way I hold my head high even when my heart is heavy. Perhaps the real victory isn't in silencing the storm but in dancing through it with courage and grace.

Now, here I am, a paradox of fear and fierceness, of trembling hands and determined steps. Even when the world makes me want to hide, I keep showing up, keep moving forward, proving to myself that, despite everything, I am still here, still standing, still strong."

I became the resting place for your burdens, yet when the tables turned, you became a fleeting guest in my trials.

The road was steep, but my feet kept moving, not towards the end, but towards becoming.

"I often find myself standing at the crossroads of solitude and company, yearning to be an outgoing spirit, the kind that flutters effortlessly from one person to another like a butterfly in a sunlit garden. Yet, whenever I'm around people, it feels like I'm walking barefoot on shards of glass—each conversation, each glance, a sting that cuts deep into my skin. I crave connection, to feel the warmth of shared laughter and stories, but the moment I step into a crowd, the weight of a thousand eyes presses down on me, and I retreat into my shell.

I feel alone, a lone tree in a desolate field, yet the idea of meeting people feels like diving into the deep end of an ocean I've never swum in, the fear of drowning in unfamiliar waters too great to bear. What is this paradox? Is it something within me, a fragment of my mind that creates a barrier where no one should exist, or is it the world that feels too sharp, too jagged against the edges of my soul? Perhaps it's both—my thoughts are a tangled web, each strand a question without an answer, and I'm caught in the middle, unable to move forward, yet too afraid to stay where I am. I wish I knew what this was, this constant push and pull, this dance between longing and fear."

I was the bridge you crossed when your usual path was blocked, but never the road you chose first.

In a world of whispers, I am a scream waiting to break free.

"The skies have a way of taking me back, don't they? Like a soft lullaby whispered by the wind, they remind me of those endless days when the world felt as vast and open as the horizon. Back when the warmth of my mother's and father's arms was like a blanket on a chilly night, wrapping me in a cocoon of safety and love."

When I think of my childhood, I see my grandparents' faces—like the sun's gentle rays breaking through a cloudy day, their love was steady, always there, warming my heart in ways only they knew how.

Now that I'm grown, the skies seem different, or maybe it's just me. We don't show our love as openly as we used to, do we? It's hidden in the

spaces between words, in the pauses of our conversations. The hugs are fewer, the playful nudges less frequent, but I know it's still there, like a river running deep beneath the surface. I

can feel it in the scoldings, in the corrections— a

love that's not loud but lingers, like an echo in a canyon.

Maybe love changes as we grow, like the seasons shift in the sky. It's no longer in the open fields of laughter and warmth but in the quiet shelter of care and concern. Then, I look to the skies and remember, knowing that even if we don't say it as often, our love still holds strong, tucked away like a cherished keepsake, just waiting for the right moment to shine through."

Every feather I find is a note in her love letter, written across the sky just for me.

The sun wasn't gone;
it was just waiting for me
To look up again.

"It's funny, isn't it, how some words can cut deeper than any blade, carving scars into places that no one else can see? The condescension in their voices, like a chilly wind on a bitter night, tries to seep into my bones, making me question my worth and dulling my spirit. They manage to find the tender spots, the ones I guard so carefully, and press just hard enough to leave a bruise that doesn't fade. Each word, like a pebble dropped into a pond, ripples through my thoughts, sending waves of doubt crashing against the shore of my heart.

But then, just when I feel those shadows creeping in, she comes to me—my maternal grandmother, like a beam of moonlight breaking through the darkest clouds. In my dreams, she wraps me in her warmth, her love spilling over me like a soft blanket on a freezing morning. From heaven, she casts her light upon me, not with words but with a feeling that radiates through every fibre of my being. Her presence is like a gentle whisper in the wind, telling me that I am worthy, that I am strong. She reminds me of all the happiness I deserve, of all the capabilities I hold within me.

And so, I rise. I rise above the hurtful words that try to pull me down, knowing that her love and blessings are like a shield, guarding me against the darkness. I live fiercely, not just for myself but for her—for the belief she had in me, for the light she still shines on me from beyond. She reminds me that no matter how deep the wounds, her love is deeper still, and it fills me with the strength to keep going, to face each day with a heart full of courage and a spirit that refuses to be dimmed."

Like a ship tossed in a storm, I navigate the harsh winds of their words, seeking my own harbour.

Not every step forward is a leap,
but every inch is still progress.

"Anxiety surges when people unveil their true colours as if they've been shedding their skin all along, leaving me to wonder—where am I standing now, and where do I go from here? The moment their masks fall, the world around me shifts, and the once-clear path dissolves into a fog of uncertainty. How do you trust the ground beneath you when it quakes with every revelation when the people you thought you knew become unrecognisable? Do I take the first step forward, or am I simply wandering in circles, searching for a direction that no longer exists? And how do I even begin to move when every turn seems like it leads deeper into confusion? It's as though the map I was

following was a mirage, and now I'm left stranded, grasping for stability in a place where the familiar feels foreign. Where do I find the courage to navigate this landscape of shifting loyalties, and how do I continue when even the act of moving feels like I'm treading on thin air, unsure if the next step will bring me closer to clarity or further into chaos?"

The whispers of the past are like echoes in a canyon, but I'm crafting my own song to fill the space.

It's like watching a sunbeam dance on the water while I am drowning in the shadows you cast.

"It's a strange kind of sorrow, watching the ones who pierced your soul with betrayal, who hurled stones in your direction, quietly slipping into the role of victimhood, as though the damage was never their doing. They carry on, unburdened, as if they've perfected the art of casting shadows while basking in the light, knowing you won't—can't—confront them. They thrive in the comfort of your silence, wearing smiles as though their conscience remains untarnished.

And there you are, standing in the rubble of their choices, aching but restrained, wondering how the truth can feel so heavy while they float so effortlessly.

But amid that sadness, a flicker of hope begins to stir, doesn't it? It's not blind hope, but the quiet, steady belief in the unseen force of karma, the idea that life has a way of balancing its scales. You start to feel the roots of resilience take hold beneath your feet. There's a shift— a realisation that their temporary victories don't define you. Slowly, you begin to believe in yourself, in your own integrity, the quiet righteousness of being true, even when the world seems indifferent to the harm they've caused.

You realise you are not defined by their actions, nor by your inability to confront them. Instead, you're shaped by the strength it takes to carry on with grace, knowing that the universe has its way of returning what is owed. They may rejoice in their illusions for now, but deep down, you sense that truth, like the quietest wind, will one day sweep through their lives. And when it does, you will still be standing—whole, right, and unshaken in your belief that you are, and always have been, on the side of what is just."

Their laughter may echo like a distant storm,
but I'm finding my own rhythm in the silence
that follows.

You wrote your goodbye in the spaces between your words, long before you left.

"I once was the kind of person whose world revolved around them, as if my existence was tethered to their very breath. It was as though my heartbeat to the rhythm of their presence, and without them, the silence was deafening. When they left, the void swallowed me whole, and for days I wept, lost in the sea of my own sadness, as though I had misplaced a piece of myself. But time, like the gentlest tide, washed over me, and slowly, without even noticing, I found my own rhythm again—one that was mine alone. Suddenly, the air felt lighter, and I could breathe deeply, freely. The happiness that bloomed within me was unfamiliar, yet pure. It was like discovering a new sky after years of looking at the same horizon.

But sometimes, in the quiet moments, when the world is still, a thought creeps in: Did I love them enough? How could I, who once couldn't imagine a day without them, now live in peace, barely remembering the shape of their absence? And then it strikes me—perhaps I did love them deeply, as deeply as I could at the time. But love is not always an eternal fire; sometimes it's a fleeting flame that burns brightly, only to die out when its purpose is fulfilled. Maybe it wasn't that I forgot them, but that I finally remembered myself. I realised that the love I gave them was never meant to keep me bound in sorrow; it was meant to teach me that I could love and still be whole, even without them."

The scars of unlovable moments are like constellations, mapping the journey to my true self.

You hold the match, but it's my heart that burns in the quiet.

"You made me question everything in the mirror that day. It wasn't just the dress I had chosen, but the way I saw myself in it. I stood there, feeling like a painting in the wrong frame, wondering if my colours were too bold for the room. Was I overdressed, or had I simply misread the canvas of the occasion? You didn't say much, but the silence in your gaze echoed louder than any words. Suddenly, I was adjusting my dress, pulling at invisible threads of doubt, asking myself if I was the odd one out in a sea of simplicity.

It felt like I was trying to wear confidence that didn't quite fit, as if the dress itself became a question mark stitched into the fabric. Am I too much? Too little? Too out of place? Every fold of the cloth seemed to weigh heavier with uncertainty. And there I was, stuck between owning my choices and wanting to disappear as if blending into the crowd would somehow silence the self-doubt that you stirred within me.

It's strange how a simple moment can make you feel like your reflection has betrayed you, leaving you unsure of whether you wore the dress or if the dress was wearing you."

Their whispers wrap around me like cobwebs,
making it hard to move freely in my own skin.

With each fall,

I grew roots.

And those roots birthed wings.

"They made me question the very fabric of who I was, as if beauty could only be defined by a checklist I had somehow never received. Every sideways glance, every whispered comment in the corners of my existence seemed to plant seeds of doubt deep within me. Who would befriend someone like you? They'd say, their words hovering like a shadow over every attempt I made to step into the light. I was labelled as a relic of an era long past, as though my preferences for something more real, something that didn't fade with trends, made me unworthy of belonging.

They measured my worth by the lens of modernity, as if authenticity was a flaw and tradition was a cage I had locked myself into. I became the 'old-school girl,' the one whose love for sincerity, whose heart beat to the rhythm of handwritten letters and slow-dancing souls, was out of sync with the fast-paced, disposable world around me. I was seen not as unique, but as outdated—someone who didn't blend but rather stood out, not in a way that commanded admiration, but in a way that drew judgement.

And yet, as they critiqued me, it became painfully clear that their words were never really about me. They were merely reflections of a society obsessed with conformity; a world afraid of those who refused to mould themselves into shallow shapes. I was not the one out of place—they were. Their opinions were nothing more than fragile constructions, and I realised that I had never been too 'traditional,' too 'different,' or too 'unblended.' I had merely been too real in a world too artificial to understand."

I've worn their doubts like a second skin, but
I'm ready to shed it for something lighter.

Beneath the rubble,
I found my voice,
and with it,
I built my way back up.

"I watched in silence as the room filled with the smoke of assumptions, each wisp carrying the lie that I was nothing but a façade—a false friend draped in a disguise of goodness. And there you stood, not as the defender I once believed you to be, but as the keeper of the match that lit the flame. I saw it in your stillness, in your quiet compliance as they tore down everything I had built with you, brick by fragile brick. Your silence wasn't the absence of words; it was the loudest confession, the final stroke in a betrayal I had never prepared for.

When I needed you, not as a saviour, but as someone who knew the truth, you were already gone—retreating into the shadows you yourself had cast. It wasn't their voices that broke me; it was yours, the one I never heard. I could have stood there, unravelling the web of lies you spun, piece by piece, but what would that have proved? I had no desire to battle over illusions when all I ever held for you was respect, woven tightly into the fabric of a friendship I cherished more than my own vindication.

I couldn't fight you, not because I lacked proof, but because what I had was far more

Delicate memories of trust, of loyalty, of moments where I had believed in us. You may have spread seeds of doubt into the world, but those seeds will wither, while what we had, real and unshakeable, will linger in your heart longer than you expect.

I wish you well, not because you deserve it, but because I was never the person they accused me of being. And one day, when the mirrors around you crack and show you the truth, you'll realise that friends like me don't simply come and go. You'll look for another, but I was never replaceable. I was the one who would have stood by you through storms you couldn't even see coming, but now, you'll weather them alone."

She was a painter of smiles, but the canvas of our bond was splattered with lies and half-truths.

I water my roots with hope, even in the drought of your absence.

"Sometimes, I feel like there's a presence in the air, a silent observer woven into the fabric of the sky, listening to the words I speak in the

stillness of my room. It's as if the air itself is a patient confidant, bending its invisible ear to catch every whispered thought and unspoken wish. No physical being is ever free to listen— to really listen without the weight of their own thoughts or the pull of their own needs. But the wind seems to understand, swirling around me with a quiet empathy, carrying my words like delicate secrets whispered into its embrace.

The sky, too, feels alive, an expansive canvas stretching over me, vast and knowing. It absorbs my every sigh, every breath, as if it were a great listener spread thin across the heavens, offering an endless expanse of understanding that no earthly soul could match. Even the inanimate things in my room—the quiet hum of the fan, the stillness of the books on my shelf—seem to lean in, attentive, cradling my confessions in their silence. I wonder if they are vessels for my thoughts, holding pieces of me in ways no human can, untouched by judgement or impatience.

There's a comfort in this invisible audience, in knowing that while no physical being can ever be truly free to listen without bias or distraction, the air, the sky, and the objects around me remain steadfast, ever-present, and ready to absorb all that I have to say. In their quiet companionship, I find a solace that transcends the limitations of human connection."

When the lights flicker, it's as if she's sending me Morse code from beyond, whispering, "I'm here."

In your gaze, I became both the question and the answer you never sought.

"Before her, I often gazed into an elusive mirror, my classmate's laughter a haunting symphony that played on repeat in my mind. With every mockery of my grades, I felt myself becoming a mere shadow, reflecting an image that was never quite enough for her discerning eyes. In her brilliance, I found myself dwarfed, each of her achievements a towering mountain I struggled to climb. Yet, as I stood before that mirror, a revelation dawned upon me: I held the power to shatter its deceptive surface. The laughter that once cut deep began to morph into a catalyst for transformation, propelling me to seek the light within myself rather than through her validation. I realised that while her accolades may shine brightly, they do not diminish the flicker of my own potential. And so, I took a step back, allowing the reflection to evolve, crafting a new narrative where I was no longer defined by her standards but instead by my unwavering journey toward self-acceptance and growth."

I felt like a marionette, strings pulled taut by the whims of other classmates.

In the mirror of her laughter, I saw a ghost of potential, distorted and trembling; yet, with every cruel jest, I polished the glass of my spirit, revealing a brilliance that would outshine her fleeting glory.

"At times, my thoughts become a labyrinth where the wounds inflicted by others' words reside like phantom pains, each memory a needle pricking anew. Their words, like barbed arrows, strike at the most vulnerable corners of my soul, and though I long to dislodge them, they are still embedded, a constant reminder of their sting. Yet, when I consider responding, I unleash my own torrent of words to defend or retaliate, a deeper impulse stays my hand, an inner voice that bids me hold my peace.

I find myself caught in the tension between what feels like weakness and what could be strength. Is my silence merely a shield for my own fear—a reluctance to expose the raw wounds they've carved into me? Or is it a profound unwillingness to inflict pain upon those who have already marred me, an instinctive refusal to perpetuate the cycle of hurt? My empathy binds me, not in softness but in a strange, unyielding fortitude that compels me to absorb the blows rather than reflect them.

This hesitation, this refusal to respond in kind, could be seen as a frailty, a lack of courage to confront and retaliate. Yet, perhaps there is a subtler form of courage in restraint, in choosing to break the chain of cruelty rather than add my own links to it. Is there not a quiet strength in choosing not to mirror the harm done to me, in holding my silence and letting the tempest pass without hurling my own thunderbolts back? Or am I simply too apprehensive, too encumbered by the fear of standing alone in opposition, even when justified?

I am ensnared in this paradox, this ceaseless oscillation between the desire to shield myself and the instinct to protect even those who have wounded me. Is this reluctance a testament to a hidden strength, a grace under pressure, or merely a manifestation of my own fear of conflict? I do not know whether this restraint is a weakness that shackles me or a strength that defines me, but it is a part of my essence that I cannot relinquish, no matter how much I sometimes wish I could."

Like shadows in the twilight, their judgements linger, but I refuse to be defined by them.

You see a flower; I see roots that can withstand any drought.

"Oh, they think I envy their dazzling escapades and glittering social life, as if I'm sitting here in the dark, wishing I could be a part of their inner circle of superficial glamour. They believe I'm yearning for the days when I was just another accessory to their self-centred stories. But the truth is, every time I see them parade around in their hollow happiness, I realise increasingly that they were never truly my friends. They were just passing actors in a play I was mistakenly cast in, thinking it was a drama of deep connection when it was always a farce of convenience. So, while they sip their cocktails and toast to their fleeting bonds, I'm toasting to my newfound clarity: I never needed to be part of their script; I'm writing my own, and it's a masterpiece of genuine connections and peace. Keep your parties and your pretence; I'll take solitude and sincerity any day."

While they twirl in a masquerade of borrowed lights, I find my own glow in the quiet corners of authenticity, crafting a narrative that needs no audience.

I learned to fear silence because it was in those quiet moments that the truth screamed the loudest :you were never really my friend. You were just someone who enjoyed watching me fall apart while pretending to help pick up the pieces.

"I walked out into the rain, thinking I could handle the drizzle of their taunts and condescending smiles. At first, it was just a few drops—small, sharp words that stung but didn't hurt much. But then, the rain picked up, turning into a downpour that soaked me to the bone.The cold settled in, and before I knew it, I was burning with a high fever—and every breath became a struggle, a cough that echoed with anxiety, reminding me of my own fragility. I could say it was the rain's fault, that the weather was cruel, but deep down, I know I was the one who stepped out without an umbrella, letting their words drench me. I let them in, didn't I? I thought I was strong enough to stand in their storm, but all it did was leave me shivering, sick, and longing for warmth that never came."

I ventured into their storm, thinking I could brave the rain, only to find it was my own heart that soaked through, leaving me cold and yearning for shelter.

Fake people left me second-guessing my worth, as if I had to earn something that should have been freely given. Now, I find myself questioning every genuine gesture, wondering if there's a hidden agenda behind every 'I care.'

"Do you remember how it used to be when we couldn't go a day without talking? Somewhere along the way, that faded, didn't it? I could feel you slipping through the cracks of our friendship, but I never wanted to admit it. You never really said goodbye, but one day I looked up, and it was like you weren't there anymore. Funny how we can sit in the same room now, and it feels like we're worlds apart. I guess I keep wondering if you miss what we had, or if you even notice how quiet things have become between us. I'm just holding on to memories.

that you've already let go of. Did you ever stop to wonder why I sometimes fall silent in your presence, or were you too busy with the noise of your own happiness? I see you, surrounded by admiration, while I stand just outside the circle, watching the world applaud you. It's not that I don't want to see you soar—it's just that sometimes, I wonder if you notice that I'm still on the ground. Do you ever feel the cold distance between us, or are you so accustomed to the warmth of everyone's attention that you've forgotten what it's like to feel alone? While you bask in the sun, I sit in the shade, wondering if you even know I'm still here."

While you revel in the spotlight, I stand in the wings, grappling with the echoes of our fading connection, hoping you still remember the warmth of shared moments.

It isn't just about fearing loneliness; it's about fearing the kind of loneliness that comes from being surrounded by people who pretend to care. It's the emptiness that hits when you realise you're truly on your own, even in a crowded room.

"What if all this time, I've been dancing to a song only I could hear? I've imagined every look, every word, every touch, thinking they were part of this melody we shared. But what if I'm the only one caught in this dance, twirling in circles under a moonlit sky they never even noticed? What if the lights in my heart that flicker every time I think of them are merely stars in my own private night, shining alone?

I've been painting a portrait of connection on a canvas they might never even glance at. And here I am, holding this gallery of memories they may not even remember, while they wander through a world where I'm just a shadow, barely an outline. What if they don't even think of me at all, and I've been the only one keeping this flame alive, while they move through their days as if I'm a breath of wind they never felt? Is it a cruel twist of fate, or just a gentle reminder to wake up from this dream I've been living?"

I've built a lighthouse of memories in a fog of solitude, shining brightly while they navigate their waters, unaware of the beacon I've become.

My life is supposed to be a garden where each flower blooms in its own way, not a neatly, trimmed hedge shaped by your hands.

"You know, it's funny how you always seemed to have these ideas about what my life should look like. Every time we talked, it felt like there was this invisible checklist I was supposed to follow—what job to get, who to marry, how to live. I never really pushed back, did I? I just nodded along, trying to be the version of myself that you wanted. But lately, I've started to wonder if you ever saw the real me, the person who didn't quite fit into your plans. It's not that I don't love you— I do. It's just that I'm starting to realise that love doesn't have to mean living up to someone else's expectations."

I've been a puppet on the strings of your dreams, but now I'm cutting the ties and learning to move to the rhythm of my own heart.

One-sided love feels like writing letters to someone who never writes back. You pour out your heart, but the mailbox stays empty, and you're left holding onto hope that maybe, just maybe, the next letter will be different.

"Isn't it strange how the sound of your voice, the simple act of seeing your name light up my screen, once felt like the universe pulling me into a soft embrace? In the chaos of my hardest days, just one message from you had the power to stitch the frayed edges of my world back together. You were my anchor, my lighthouse in the storm, and I clung to the warmth of your care like a lifeline. But when I was left stranded in the very storms I thought you'd help me weather, I realised how fragile that lifeline was—how it unravelled, leaving me adrift.

And yet, even in that darkness, the weight of your absence pressing down on me, it wasn't anger or bitterness that filled my heart. No, it was guilt—guilt that gnawed at me, whispering questions I didn't know how to silence. 'Did I' hurt you?' I wondered. 'What could I have done differently? How must you be feeling?' As if somehow, the ache you left me with was my burden to justify. Even when I was the one bleeding, I convinced myself that maybe it was my fault for not bandaging your wounds. It's maddening, how I could be the one shattered, yet still worry about the pieces of you.

I suppose that's the kind of person I've always been—constantly searching for fault in myself, even when the cracks in my heart were caused by the very person I trusted to protect it. But there comes a point where even the kindest heart tyres of carrying the weight of other people's shadows. And perhaps that's what I'm learning now – that sometimes, the ones who leave you stranded are the ones who never really knew how to stay. And in that knowing, I might finally start choosing my own healing over the endless questioning of what I did wrong."

I was a shipwrecked sailor, clinging to your driftwood, but now I'm learning to build my own vessel, ready to navigate the storms on my own terms.

I used to believe in the purity of love and friendship until reality showed me, they are often tainted with jealousy, lies, and selfishness.

"Amidst the intricate mosaic of our shared journey, I've often found myself an outlier, an solitary star casting light in a sky enamoured with shadows. My mind, an unruly ocean of creativity, has stirred both admiration and unease in you—do you recall those moments when you saw me, torn between envy and curiosity? I, the tempestuous artist, danced while you anchored yourself in the harbour of the familiar. Yet, as fate would have it, your whispered dreams have recently blossomed into vivid realities. Was it not the spark of my imagination that nudged you to venture beyond the confines of your own world? If this transformation had not unfolded, would I have still been a fleeting wisp in your thoughts, a ghost haunting the edges of your carefully constructed life? What if our paths, woven together by threads of creativity and aspiration, were always destined to converge?"

I've been the brush that splattered creativity on your canvas, yet as your dreams take flight, I can't help but question if I was meant to be a vibrant addition or just a passing flicker.

You were the anchor that weighed me down,
mistaking your comfort for stability while
I fought to stay afloat in turbulent waters.

"Life, we need to sit down for a heart-to-heart.

You've been the architect of my journey, sketching out blueprints for paths I never wished to walk. You handed me a job that feels like a weighty anchor, dragging me into waters that suffocate my spirit. I followed your map, believing it would lead to a treasure I now realise is buried beneath the sands of routine.

Each day, I don a mask, performing a role in a play where I've lost my lines, yearning for the vibrant colours of my own dreams that have faded in the backdrop of your expectations.

You've spun my choices into a web of security, but what about the wild threads of passion that have been left untangled? It's time to dismantle this façade and reclaim the brush, painting my own canvas with the hues of authenticity. I refuse to be a mere character in your script; I'm ready to direct my own story."

I'm ready to break free from your design and create a masterpiece that truly reflects who I am.

You've charted my course for too long; now it's my turn to navigate the seas of my own desires.

"In the midst of life's relentless flow, I find myself wrestling with the thought of where you are now. We used to paint our days with laughter and shared secrets, two artists exploring the same canvas of imagination. Yet, somehow, we drifted into separate galleries, each facing our own struggles. I often wonder how the vibrant colours of our friendship faded into the background, and if you, too, carry the weight of those memories. Do you ever take a moment to reflect on what we had, or has the passage of time pulled you so far forward that the past feels like a distant echo? It's a challenge to reconcile the joy we once shared with the distance that now separates us, leaving me to ponder if our paths will ever intertwine again."

Sometimes, as life rushes by, I catch myself reminiscing about our laughter and wonder if you miss those moments as much as I do.

Do you ever glance back at our shared moments, or have they become like forgotten stars in the vastness of your sky?

"Do you ever consider the weight of your words, how they crashed over me like a tempest, whispering 'you are nothing,' until I felt like a mere seedling struggling to survive? Did you know that your disbelief could bend my branches but not break my spirit? Each time you dismissed my potential, did you realise you were sowing seeds of doubt deep within me?

Yet, in that storm, I found the courage to stretch toward the light, to transform your harsh winds into the very force that helped me grow. Can you see now that those storms shaped me into something resilient, something beautiful, capable of blooming despite the desolation? I emerged not as the nothing you proclaimed, but as a testament to survival and strength, reaching for the sun in a way you never expected."

Carved from the stone of their derision, I emerged as a masterpiece in progress; with every chisel of criticism, I shaped my own form, transforming the rough edges into a sculpture that tells the story of my perseverance.

Your words were the storm clouds that shadowed my potential, yet I emerged as a rainbow, vibrant and resilient.

"Amongst them, I often played the role of a shadow, trailing in the wake of their laughter and accomplishments. Their brilliance shone like a radiant sun, illuminating paths I longed to traverse, while I felt like a muted silhouette, forever eclipsed by their radiance. Each shared moment was a reminder of my place in their world—a position of lesser significance, where my own light struggled to break through the veneer of their expectations. Yet, in that shadowy existence, I began to discover an unexpected strength. Shadows, I learned, have their own form of beauty, dancing gracefully in the corners where light dares not tread. I realised that rather than coveting their brilliance, I could create my own luminous dance, illuminating the spaces they overlooked.

Embracing my identity as both a shadow and a light, I carved out a unique path where I could flourish, celebrating the subtlety of my existence while acknowledging that even in darkness, there is potential for illumination."

Each sound of laughter echoed like the tolling of a distant bell, a reminder that I was but a phantom in their light; yet, as I stood at the edge of their brilliance, I ignited a fire within that illuminated my own path.

You made sure to make me feel like chasing phantoms in a carnival of brilliance, your laughter, a haunting reminder of my own perceived inadequacies.

Until Next Time

Dear Reader,

I have been through many storms, and maybe you have too. Perhaps that is why you are

holding this book in your hands. You're seeking words that reflect your hidden aches, the unsaid feelings that linger quietly beneath the surface. Maybe, like me, you have faced rejection, betrayal, the weight of expectations, or the sting of not being enough for someone you once held dear. And if so, I want to tell you—my heart recognises yours.

Growing up, I was always the one standing on the outside. I felt the glances, the side comments that weren't always meant to hurt but managed to do so anyway. People see differences and

draw their lines in the sand, and it's easy to get lost on the wrong side of those lines. Maybe you know what I mean—maybe you've been that "odd one out," too. Whether it was your appearance, your opinions, or simply the fact

that you didn't fit into the box others had made for you, they made sure you felt it. That feeling of never quite belonging can cling to you, like an invisible cloak that makes you wonder if

you'll never be enough.

I've been there. I've stood in that shadow, aching for a little warmth, a little recognition.

But what I didn't realise at the time, what I

couldn't see through the haze of hurt, was that those shadows were shaping me. They were giving me the space to find my fire, the place to nurture a determination so fierce it would one day set my whole path ablaze. Each moment of doubt they cast on me became fuel for my ambition. The walls they built around me gave me something to climb, something to overcome, and I did.

If you are still in that place—feeling like the world doesn't see you for who you are, or worse, that it's actively pushing you away—I hope you find solace in these words. I hope you know that it's in those very moments of rejection that your true strength is born. You see, adversity is a funny thing; it feels like a weight, but in truth, it's a force that helps you rise.

But of course, none of us gets through life unscathed. There are other pains, more personal ones, that cut deeper because they come from those we love and trust. When a friend who feels like a sister turns her back on you, when she betrays you in ways you never imagined, it leaves a scar that words can't quite heal. It's the kind of wound that makes you question everything—your choices, your worth, your ability to trust again.

I've been through that, too. And I wish I could tell you that time erases the hurt, but it doesn't. What time does, though, is give you distance, perspective. It helps you understand that their betrayal is not a reflection of you—it's a reflection of them. And in the end, it frees you. It gives you the chance to grow, to move forward without the weight of their expectations, without the need for their approval. You get to choose your own path, one that is no longer tethered to the people who tried to hold you back.

And then there's the silent ache of expectations. The ones we place on ourselves, the ones our families place on us. You know the feeling, don't you? That unspoken pressure to be something, someone—a success, a perfect version of yourself that never stumbles, never falters. The truth is, those expectations can weigh more than any rejection. They sit on your chest, making it hard to breathe, hard to see clearly. But what I've learned—what I hope you are learning, too—is that you don't owe anyone perfection. You don't owe anyone an explanation for who you are or the choices you make. Your journey is your own, and the only person you need to impress is yourself.

As I write this, I know that many of you reading these words have faced struggles that echo my own. You've felt the pang of isolation, the sting of betrayal, the crushing weight of unspoken expectations. You've fought battles within yourself that no one else could see, and yet, here you are—still standing, still moving forward. It aches my heart to think of the pain you might have endured, but it also fills me with pride, because you survived. You found a way to keep going, even when it felt impossible.

But let's be honest—survival leaves its mark.

The things we've faced, they don't just

don't disappear once we've overcome them. They linger, like shadows on a sunny day. And those shadows, those unsaid feelings, are what we carry with us. We don't always have the words to express them, but they live inside us, shaping who we are and how we move through the world.

As you read through the pages of this book, I hope you find a piece of yourself here. I hope my words offer a reflection of your own journey, a mirror that shows you that you are not alone. And, most of all, I hope these stories, these moments of adversity and triumph, bring you deserve comfort. Because you deserve it. Your heart deserves to rest, to find solace in knowing that, despite everything, you have always been enough.

I won't pretend that reading these words will fix everything. It won't erase the scars or fill the empty spaces left by those who have hurt you. But I do hope it offers you a kind of peace, a reminder that you are stronger than you know, and that even in the quiet moments of doubt, you are worthy of love and light.

I'll leave you with this, a rhyme to carry with you:

"In the darkest moments, when silence falls,

And the weight of the world feels like stone walls,

Remember the light that still burns inside, A fire that no storm can hide.

You are the sun after the rain. The strength born from all the pain. So, when life tries to pull you apart, hold fast to the power in your heart."

I believe in you, dear reader. More than you know.

Other Titles By Sneha Jain

- *The Visionary Lights from a Dark Mind*
- *She – The Withered Flower*
- *The Jewels of Elegance*
- *The Wind and the Grit*
- *Be the First You*
- *Threads of Life: Stories Woven from Ordinary Moments*
- *The Lone Trailblazer*

www.ingramcontent.com/pod-product-compliance
Lightning Source LLC
LaVergne TN
LVHW090123160826
845673LV00015B/828
* 9 7 9 8 8 9 5 8 8 6 9 8 4 *